Dolls and Dolls Houses

Kay Desmonde

Dolls and Dolls Houses

Crescent Books ● New York

Contents

6

Dolls and Dolls Houses

INTRODUCTION

Dolls which were the Cinderellas of collectable antiques are now, after a very slow start, becoming increasingly sought after by collectors. In the past beautiful and interesting old dolls were often taken to the United States, where doll collecting has been the second most popular hobby for many years. Fortunately there are many lovely old dolls still to be found, so new collectors can start, confidently knowing they will be able to assemble a varied and worthwhile collection. It is with these new collectors in mind that I have compiled this book and the dolls illustrated were all available for sale at the time of writing. Although this book is primarily for beginners it is hoped that the plates will be of value to the more advanced collector too.

There are many other excellent books available on this subject and these I have listed in the Bibliography (see page 80). The most comprehensive is, in my opinion, *The Collector's Encyclopedia of Dolls* by Mrs. Dorothy Coleman, a charming American lady who has condensed a lifetime's research into the history of all types of dolls in this book, without which all doll enthusiasts would be infinitely the poorer.

Anyone starting to collect old dolls should begin by looking at as many different dolls as possible, in museums and in private collections. If the local museum has only a few on display ask if they have any in the archives you can see. Some museums put few on display thinking they are of little interest in comparison with their rarer and more valuable antiquities, but, because of their very personal appeal, many people in the past have given their childhood treasures to museums feeling unable to throw them away or leave them knowing the dolls would be similarly disposed of on their death. Having seen as many different types of doll as possible the new collector should then decide what kind of doll to collect. Large dolls require large houses and flat dwellers may wish to collect the miniature dolls of which there are many varieties, some of exquisite quality. Often collectors begin by seeing a doll similar to one owned as a child and on buying it they relive the childhood happiness they once experienced on owning such a treasure. A doll is usually a child's most valued possession, a comfort in distress or loneliness, the feeling for which can never be superseded by later and more valuable possessions. Apart from this personal appeal a doll is not only a child's toy, it is a representation of the period in which it was produced and there are many interesting sidelines to doll collecting, for example, the history of costume, which includes the materials used for various clothes and the colours which were fashionable at various times as well as the actual fashions of the clothes; the history of the country from which the dolls originate; the types of dolls made according to the availability of the various materials used; finding paintings of children with dolls; reading books and magazines of the period; and so on until the whole subject becomes a fascination.

Early Dolls

In a book of this size it is impossible to mention all the dolls which would be worthwhile additions to any collection, but I have endeavoured to give as much variety as possible starting with the earliest dolls still obtainable. Not many dolls survive from earlier than the 18th century, but we must not overlook the fact that many wonderful dolls were made then. In 1700 there were wax babies which could cry and turn their heads and eyes, and in 1737 walking dolls were being made in Paris, but the earliest collectable doll which has survived from this era is the Queen Anne type doll. A surprisingly large number of these do still exist. Being made of wood they are practically indestructible and some have been played with by succeeding generations of children of a family up to the present day, often keeping the same name throughout. I have one on which every child who inherited it embroidered her initials on the under garments. These dolls have been well loved as they are solid enough for a child

to hold comfortably and their homely features do have charm.

It is almost impossible to accurately date the early dolls. The large doll (22 inches) illustrated on the frontispiece is believed to be pre-1700. It has carved features and painted eyes. The legs which are shaped are jointed at the hip only. Some of the earliest dolls were of very fine craftsmanship and much more elaborately jointed than the later ones which were made in greater quantities. I have hesitated to give names to dolls which are not clearly marked on the head. Where certain known characteristics of a maker are outstanding I have attributed the type to him or her. The earliest dolls were not marked at all, they were either home-made or bought at fairs which from the Middle Ages were held in different parts of the country and on the continent too. Goods which were not made in the immediate neighbourhood could be bought or bartered for there. Toys were always an important part of the display and it was very exciting for the children for they never saw toys on display except at these fairs and on the trays of itinerant pedlars. The great event in London was the Bartholomew Fair which was held in Smithfield. It was held annually from the 12th century on St. Bartholomew's Day, August 24th. Dolls sold at the fair were called Bartholomew Babies. The word 'doll' has only been used since the end of the 17th century and the derivation is unknown; but it could possibly be a name (doll is the diminutive of Dorothy) given to a doll by a pedlar who was shouting his wares and thus adopted into general usage. Today some collectors call themselves plangonologists. This is derived from the classical Greek word 'plangon' which means doll.

Pedlar Dolls

Although pedlars were known all over Europe the Pedlar Doll is uniquely British. They were made from the late-18th century onwards, the first ones being completely home-made. Often the pedlar's head was made from a dried and shrivelled apple mounted on a stick and painted. Cork, carved to shape, was also used for heads and later the mass-produced wooden and wax dolls were used. A lot of the tiny items used to fill a pedlar's tray or basket could be bought in shops but the Victorians loved to make the very tiny wares themselves. The tiniest of socks imaginable, knitted on fine pins and with turned heels are a feature of pedlar trays. One very fine pedlar doll I had was stocked with over three hundred miniature items including Wedgwood vases and Nailsea glass—and a tiny dolls' house.

Marked Dolls

Occasionally wax dolls have their maker's name, but it was not until the latter part of the 19th century that the bisque dolls' heads were impressed with either the maker's name or initials. Dolls having increased in value in recent years some now have fake marks stamped on them, so it is advisable to learn all one can about each make of doll. Look well at the face, the eyes, and the different types of bodies which went with different heads, and do not be misled by newly stamped makers' names on the doll.

There were thousands of different makers of dolls and I am constantly amazed at the number of new and un-catalogued dolls which come to light, some of which it is impossible to get any information about. Whenever possible try to discover the history of purchases. Has it always been in the same family? What has it been called and any unusual and interesting story in connection with the doll. Some stories one hears about treasured dolls are delightful, some are macabre. I once questioned the apparent newness of a 'Pumpkin' headed doll and was shown the card that went with the doll—'This doll was given to Mary Anne the night before she died, aged two years, 1865'. It had been placed in a sealed dome on her grave but later removed.

Papier Maché Heads

If one wanted a very specialist collection of dolls I can think of none better than the wide range of papier maché heads. These dolls' heads were made from the 17th century but it was not until the early-19th century that they were mass produced in Europe. These dolls are re-nowned for their different hairstyles, some very outlandish, and they are more easily dated than the earlier dolls for the elaborate hairstyles were often very short-lived. The bodies and clothes of these dolls are frequently of very poor quality but they are worth collecting for the heads alone. The first doll to be patented in the United States was the Greiner which had a papier maché head. Unfortunately these dolls are rarely found in England. The early English papier maché heads are on home-made bodies and they have very distinctive coiffures. Later ones were smaller and neater with kid bodies, and these are often found with their original hand-made clothes in exceptionally good condition, so one assumes that this doll, the first kind to be produced in large quantities, was often the most treasured possession of its little owner and kept under a glass dome, hence the wonderful state of preservation that is a feature of these dolls. Papier maché is known to have been used in France for making dolls' heads since 1540 and in Germany from the beginning of the 19th century. The words *holz-masse* which are sometimes printed on later dolls' bodies is the German for wood pulp of which the bodies were made.

Peg Wooden Dolls

About this period the peg wooden dolls were also being mass-produced. The early ones are extremely well modelled. They were made in all sizes but the larger ones have mostly survived. These have spoon shaped hands and long flat feet and are the dolls known as Dutch Dolls. 'Dutch' is a corruption of *Deutsch* which means German. These dolls were retailed through agents in Germany although they were produced in the Grodner Thal district of Austria. Some of these dolls have combs carved in the tops of their heads and they have curls painted round their faces. I have had them as small as $\frac{1}{2}$ an inch and have had them completely dressed from $\frac{3}{4}$ inch. At the Great Exhibition in 1851 a tiny jointed doll was sold in a wooden egg. It was labelled 'The smallest doll in the world', is $\frac{3}{4}$ inch tall and is jointed at elbows, hips and knees. By the end of the 19th century the quality of the peg wooden dolls was very poor and today one has to beware of reproductions.

Wax over Composition Dolls

The early wax over composition dolls are great favourites of mine. Their faces, although now cracked and crazed, have a charm all their own with their bright glass eyes and smiling mouths. Some of these dolls had their hair inserted in a slit at the top of their head and some had closing eyes which were operated by a wire which went through the body and came out at the side. The early ones all have corkscrew curls and are very appealing. The heads were made of papier maché, the features were painted on and then the heads were dipped in wax several times giving the doll a lovely soft glowing look.

China Heads

China dolls' heads were made before 1840 but the majority to be found today are from this date. The earliest ones were made by the finest porcelain factories, e.g. Meissen and Royal Copenhagen, and these are usually the most beautiful, showing the differing hairstyles of the period. The early ones are usually of what is known to doll collectors as lustre china (china with a pinkish glow), the later ones being of white china. The hair is usually black and the painted eyes usually blue and to find variations of these colours would make a very valuable addition to any collection. Occasionally one does find these china heads with glass eyes and very, very rarely with teeth.

The heads are on a shoulder plate which is attached to a cloth body through eyelet holes. Some china heads are to be found on kid bodies and occasionally on wooden bodies. The china heads were often sold separately and were attached to a body, frequently a home-made cloth one, at home. China is pottery which is baked and glazed, bisque or 'parian' is unglazed china (see below). These china heads were mostly made in Germany and there are many interesting and collectable variations. Some have collars, jewellery or embroidery moulded on their shoulder plates. Some have ornamentation in the hair—snoods, flowers, feathers, combs, ribbons, jewels—and there are also the bonnet heads. China heads continued to be made until the 1920s but the later styles were plainer and of very poor quality. China dolls were made in all sizes from dolls' house size up to 36 inches. The later dolls had shorter and plumper necks and it is helpful in dating these dolls to remember to look at the legs and, if these are original, the flat heeled painted shoes are the earlier ones. High heels were re-introduced into Europe in 1860 and these were copied on the dolls, which usually quite closely followed changes in fashion.

Unglazed Dolls

Contemporary with the earlier china headed dolls were dolls with similar hair styles and ornamentation made in papier maché and bisque. These bisque dolls are sometimes called parian. True parian is, as the name suggests, like marble and white and was mostly used for making statuettes in Victorian times. These early unglazed china dolls were equally as beautiful as the glazed china ones, but they usually had blonde hair, some of them also had glass eyes and moulded bonnets. The later ones were much coarser and had a sugary appearance. Some of the heads were partly glazed to highlight various features, for example the hair or a neck ornamentation, and sometimes these are finished in pink or gold lustre. Some of the dolls have lustre boots.

The Wax Doll

Until the 1850s most of the dolls typified the young adult but at the 1851 Great Exhibition in London Madame Montanari showed wax dolls representing all ages, the baby dolls being very much admired. These dolls had real hair and eyelashes inserted into the wax and were very lifelike. Some collectors are wary of including wax dolls in their collections for they have heard heartbreaking stories from elderly relatives of wax dolls being melted out of recognition by mischievous brothers who held the dolls in front of the fire to annoy their sisters. Actually wax dolls will withstand all normal room temperatures. It is advisable not to put them in a window in direct sunlight, for even if they didn't melt the colouring would probably fade, and one must not put them immediately in front of a fire, but otherwise they are probably just as durable as the bisque dolls. At the time they were made they were sometimes stamped as warranted to withstand any climate. Many wax dolls in Victorian times were taken to outposts of the Empire by little girls accompanying their parents who worked overseas. There were many well-known wax doll-makers in London at this time and they all made superb quality dolls, many of which have fortunately survived until today. Some of the dolls have name stamps on their body, sometimes the maker's name and sometimes the name of the shop selling the dolls. A few Pierotti dolls are signed in the wax on the back of the head.

French Fashion Dolls

1860 was the beginning of a wonderful era in doll-making. The tinted bisque dolls, now called the French fashion dolls, came into vogue. These shoulder heads were on wood or kid bodies and had real hair wigs. The first ones had fixed necks but in 1861 Mlle. Huret patented a swivel neck doll which enabled the head to be moved into more naturalistic positions. These were lady type dolls and were usually dressed in the fashion of the day. At this period there were shops in Paris which sold only accessories for these beautiful dolls. The ambition of a little girl owning one of these dolls would be to furnish a trunk of fashionable clothes and accessories. These included hats, fans, gloves, eyeglasses, jewellery, furs, writing and sewing cases, and in the case of a bride doll, items for her home were also suitably boxed and sold together with the trousseau. These dolls are sometimes called 'Parisiennes' and are believed to have been made solely as luxury children's toys and not as mannequins for which earlier dolls had been used before fashion magazines were printed. There were many famous makers of these luxury dolls; among them you will find the names of Jumeau, Rohmer, Huret, Simonne, Bereux, Gaultier. The French became the popular doll-makers of the day superseding Germany who, until then, had monopolised the market. The Germans made an attempt to copy these desirable French dolls but it was not until the 1890s that they overtook the French in the doll business. Meanwhile the French had perfected a ball-jointed body and whereas the fashion dolls had been called *poupées*, the new jointed doll was called a *bébé*, although they were not actually babies but little girls. Jumeau, Bru, Steiner, Schmitt, Pannier were some of the famous names in this era of superlative quality in doll-making.

It was a luxury market and these dolls were the playthings of well-to-do children. They usually had closed mouths, and stationary, beautiful glass eyes which were specially made and had a depth to them which gave them a very realistic appearance. Bru at this time made many novelty or surprise dolls, which could suck, walk, talk, sleep or breathe. This was the era of rapid advances in the manufacture of dolls.

The German Doll-Makers

From 1890 onwards the Germans regained the market and having copied the French *bébés* they sold them at a much more reasonable price so that they became available to many more children. They made dolls with sleeping eyes worked by counterweights, open mouths with teeth and walking and talking dolls, as well as the two- and three-faced novelty dolls. Later the eyes had eyelashes and moving bisque tongues. The German companies went from strength to strength as the French doll-makers went through difficult times. By 1899 many of the famous French factories could no longer keep going on their own and they amalgamated to form the *Société Française de Fabrication de Bébés et Jouets*, known afterwards by its initials S.F.B.J. The Germans continued to flourish until World War I and this is usually the date at which the antique doll collector ends her collection, but I have included a few interesting dolls of the 1920s which would give added variety.

Dolls' Houses

In the latter part of this book I have attempted to show a few of the different types of dolls' houses available for the beginner collector today. The range of dolls' houses and furnishings is probably almost as vast as the range of dolls and I could not possibly do it justice, but if this small contribution can encourage more enthusiasts to restore and preserve these treasures of Victorian nurseries, then it is worth while.

The restoration and furnishing of antique dolls' houses is a rapidly growing hobby and it has far more male enthusiasts than doll collecting. What makes this hobby so very enjoyable is that it can be a family one, with each member contributing something, and enjoying the whole. One can repair furniture, another make curtains and weave carpets and another dress dolls and they can all search for the tiny treasures with which to furnish their houses. Victorian dolls' houses were play houses and in some cases succeeding owners have added, and taken away, wallpaper, furniture and dolls, so a large Victorian house could take years of work if one wanted to restore it to its original condition. Most collectors will have to compromise and do only the work necessary to make it pleasing to themselves. One has always to remember that one is restoring and not renovating. It is always preferable to strip off the thick coats of paint added over the years and get down to the original than to paint a nice new coat of paint over the old!

Museums all over the world have examples of fine early dolls' houses and it is fortunate that we can see and enjoy them still. The early English houses were called baby houses and were usually large and beautifully made. These replaced the earlier cupboard houses which had been furnished with collections of precious miniatures made from gold, silver, ivory, wood and china. There had been a craze for collecting among the wealthy and some of the items were very costly so all the early houses had locks for the protection of these treasures.

From about the time Queen Victoria ascended the throne the baby house ceased to be a luxury, it became a nursery toy. Wooden furniture and china were mass-produced for these houses and as the elegance of the Georgian era receded the little rooms were crammed with the furnishings in imitation of the homes of that period. Victorian dolls' houses always look better over-furnished, thereby evoking the cluttered feeling of a Victorian home.

Dating a Dolls' House

It is almost impossible to date accurately a dolls' house for which one has not obtained the previous history. Houses were built similar in type to the one the maker lived in, and how many of us live in an ultra-modern house? So one assumes they were built in a style of ten, twenty, or even fifty years earlier. Sometimes of course the house is clearly dated, but then again that does not always indicate the date the dolls' house was built, but could quite easily be the date of the house of which the plaything was a copy.

Having decided to the best of one's ability to what era one's house belongs, then one has to study the furniture of the period so that one can collect items which will suit the house. As with dolls, it is better to see as many dolls' houses as possible before deciding what to collect. It is easier to furnish to the scale of 1 inch to the foot than any other scale, but a tiny house for which one has to search and search to find the furnishings to scale can be a very worthwhile and rewarding task.

Types of Furnishings

The most eagerly sought-after furniture is what is known to collectors as 'Duncan Phyfe'. This is made of imitation rosewood with gold decoration. It was made in at least three different sizes and some of these pieces are very attractive and desirable. A lot of the later mass-produced Victorian dolls' house furniture was heavier looking but it was well made and is worth looking for. Edwardian dolls' house furniture is more easily found and this can be very useful for the minor rooms of a large house if one has not unlimited money to spend. Unfortunately there are no illustrations of the different types of furniture in this book so one will have to refer to the excellent reference books already written on dolls' houses and their contents.

The Dolls' House Family

Dolls' houses must always have a family and, if possible, visiting friends and relatives, to give them a lived-in look. One can arrange them to form a picture story; a coming-of-age party, a homecoming after a war, or any arrangement that will add interest. One of the most

charming I have seen was a small dolls' house which 'was the home of an impoverished lady who had to take in sewing to eke out her meagre income'. There she sits labouring over her tiny sewing machine. One dolls' house which I can never have too many invitations to see is owned by a friend who changes the arrangement of her house to suit the seasons. The trunk is being packed for the annual holiday, the cricket bat standing in the hall, and at Christmas there is a Christmas party with a miniature tree and the toboggan hanging in the hall ready for the snow. The enjoyment to be derived from collecting dolls' houses is endless.

I hope the following pages of photographs of dolls and dolls' houses will give pleasure and be informative to the new collector and the experienced. As I have written earlier, this book only touches very briefly on the vast variety of dolls which have been made over the years, and on the vast subject of dolls' house collecting.

I wish all collectors many happy and rewarding hours with their dolls and houses and I would like to thank all who have in the past researched so carefully into the history of dolls and dolls' houses and have generously published the facts so that we can all share the knowledge. Without these facts collecting would not be the fascinating and absorbing hobby that so many of us enjoy today.

2 Queen Anne Type Doll

This doll is 17 inches tall and believed to be English c. 1745. The head and body are carved wood, the head and shoulders being covered in gesso and then enamelled. The original wig of either flax or real hair has been replaced but the original hand-made nails are still in the head. The eyes are of blown glass, dark brown and without pupils. The eyebrows are a series of small painted dots and the eyes are also ringed by similar painted dots. The cheeks are bright pink. The back of the doll is flat and the wooden legs are jointed. The original leather arms have been replaced by ones of white kid. The doll is dressed in a fawn embroidered silk dress over a quilted petticoat. Two pockets are tied around the waist on tapes between the dress and the petticoat with access through slits in the dress. To emphasise the fashionable silhouette of the period a thick pad of quilted material is tied under the petticoat and this was known as a 'bum roll'. This type of doll would be a very desirable addition to any doll collection and is one of the earliest to be found outside museums.

More early dolls were made of wood than any other material. It was easy and cheap to obtain. Cloth was far more valuable and was not used often for dolls until the Victorian era. The type of doll illustrated was made in England where wood turners made and painted their own dolls. On the continent at this time, the guilds (the early trade unions) would not allow a turner to paint his doll, bismuth painters did this.

One way of differentiating the earlier-18th-century doll from the later is to see the shape of the base of the torso. The early ones were square and the later ones pointed. The English heads were proportionately larger than the continental ones and they also had wigs.

4 Rare Papier Maché Head
(right)

This is a very rare type of head c. 1825 with asymmetrical hairstyle, the hair being braided and taken over a comb, and curls painted on the forehead. The head is on a very deep yoke with moulded bustline. The doll has turquoise blue eyes and a lovely complexion. The body with the tiny waist is made of stuffed calico with very long cloth legs and turned-in feet. The arms are of blue leather with separated fingers. She is wearing a printed cotton dress and is 25 inches tall.

3 Wooden Dolls

The largest doll is 22 inches tall. She was well made c. 1850 and has spoon hands and long flat feet. She is jointed at shoulders, elbows, hips and knees.

The next doll is one of the later peg wooden dolls with straight hands and small red painted feet. She is 9 inches tall and was dressed for a village fair in 1888. She is in remarkably good condition having been wrapped and put away until I bought her in 1970.

The smartly dressed wooden doll in the middle is 5 inches tall and was made about 1830. She has a long neck, sloping shoulders and traces of a comb on her head.

The next one (c. 1850) is interesting because she is fully dressed, including long drawers, yet she is only 1 inch tall. She is jointed at the shoulders, elbows, hips and knees.

The little undressed doll is similar to the above but she is only $\frac{1}{2}$ an inch tall and is not jointed at the elbows.

16

5 Milliner's Model (*left*)

This shoulder head is on a very narrow waisted unjointed kid body. The arms are of wood with scoop hands and the wooden legs have flat feet with yellow painted slippers. She is 12 inches tall and was made about 1830. This is the type of doll often called a 'Milliner's Model' and occasionally thought of as an early fashion doll, but these were the first mass-produced dolls and were made at a time when it was first recognised that children needed to play and not behave as miniature adults from infancy, so they were most probably made simply as play dolls. This doll is in unusually fine condition, the clothes are all original, printed cotton dress, flannel and cotton petticoats and drawers.

6 Wax over Composition Doll

c. 1835, she is 16½ inches tall. The body is made of stuffed calico, the arms are of pink leather with separated fingers. The eyes are dark brown and pupil-less. The composition head was painted before waxing and the lovely bloom on the cheeks is still perfect. The 'crazing' on this doll's face is caused by the differing expansion and contraction rates of the wax and composition, which causes cracking during changes in temperature and humidity. This 'crazing' does not detract from the charm of these early dolls. The clothes are original, the underwear handsewn and the silk dress hand embroidered. A card came with this doll which reads, 'Doll Albenia. A present from Lady Whitcombe to Susanna Purnell before 2 years old'. The card is lined with the silk of the dress.

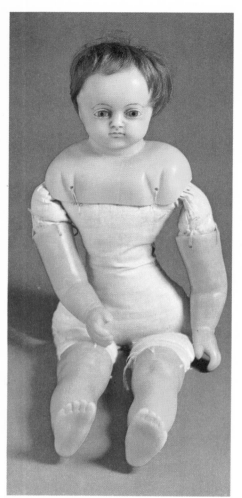

7 Montanari Type Wax Doll

Although this doll is unmarked she is typical of the known Montanari dolls. Dated c. 1860, she is about 22″ tall and has a mouth which turns down slightly at the corners. The eyes are of blue glass and the light brown hair is inserted singly into the wax. The upper and lower eyelids are well defined and still have traces of the original inserted eyelashes. Hair is also inserted in the eyebrows. The head, shoulders and limbs are very well modelled. This doll has hand-embroidered underwear and a long, hand-stitched baby gown but has been undressed to show the hand-sewn linen body which is typical of the poured wax dolls of this period.

These poured wax dolls are sometimes erroneously called solid wax dolls. A poured wax doll head is made by pouring liquid wax into a warm mould. Some only have a thin wax coating but the majority are of thick wax and these are the dolls which when finished seem to have the quality of living flesh. These dolls were originally priced from ten shillings to five guineas undressed and were considerably more fully dressed so they were dolls for the well-to-do child.

Madame Augusta Montanari was the wax doll-maker of this period and her address is listed as 29 Upper Charlotte Street, Fitzroy Square, London, W.1. Madame Montanari also made beautiful rag dolls.

8 Pierotti Doll

English poured wax doll c. 1860. This doll is exceptional as it is one of the very few wax dolls which can be accurately attributed to a maker. 'Pierotti' is written in the wax high on the back of the neck under the hair. The beautiful glass eyes are pale blue and the blonde real hair is inserted into the wax singly. The doll is 20 inches long and is dressed in hand-made baby type clothes. The attractive bonnet is of the style worn by little boys. The Pierotti family were of Italian origin and came to England in the late-18th century. They were all wax doll-makers and the women of the family made the cloth bodies for the dolls. The dolls were of an extremely high quality with rooted brows and lashes. The wax arms and legs were well modelled. Charles Ernest Pierotti, the last member of the family to make wax dolls, finally retired in 1935.

9 Poured Wax Doll

C. 1865, this doll has the 'Cremer' mark on the front of her body. She is 20 inches tall, with long blonde inserted hair, and blue glass eyes. She is in an exceptionally fine state of preservation with the original bloom still on her cheeks, and she is wearing hand-made original clothes with the original pink ribbon trimming. She has inserted eyebrows and eyelashes and this is possibly a Pierotti doll as Henry Cremer who had one of the finest toy shops in London at 210 Regent Street is known to have used Pierotti heads on his dolls. Such a pretty little doll must have been a wonderful gift to some small Victorian girl.

10 China Head Doll

c. 1840. Sometimes known as the 'covered wagon' doll because of her hairstyle. She is 23 inches long and has blue painted eyes with the red line over. Her shoulders slope deeply and she is attached to the cotton body through two eyelet holes in the front and in the back of the shoulder plate. The black painted boots have flat heels and inside lacing. There is a red painted bow just below each knee. She has her original white cotton drawers and petticoat and a blue and white chequered silk dress. She is a pink lustre china doll, but she has photographed as if she were the later white china type.

12 Parian Type Doll (*right*)

c. 1865. She is 14 inches tall and has a hard stuffed cotton body. The blue painted eyes have the red line over and her cheeks appear very highly coloured against the untinted bisque. The moulded hair is painted a blonde colour and is arranged in vertical sausage curls all round. The arms and legs are un-glazed and the black painted boots have small heels. She is wearing her original blue print dress and white cotton under-wear.

11 China Head Doll

c. 1865. She is $16\frac{1}{2}$ inches long and has a deep shoulder line with two holes back and front through which it is stitched to the hard stuffed cotton body with the tiny waist. This doll has very pale colouring and a pleasant expression, but is not made of pink lustre china. The blue painted eyes have a red line above. The legs have pink bows below the knees and the black painted boots have small heels. All round the head are well modelled vertical sausage curls.

13 Blue Scarf Doll

Fine quality bisque doll c. 1870. The head is believed to have been a copy of a portrait of the Empress Louise of Prussia descending the stairs at the Schönbrunn Palace to intercede with Napoleon on behalf of her country. The doll has blue eyes with a red line painted above. The long fair curls and scarf are finely moulded bisque. She has delicately tinted bisque arms and legs which have brown side-buttoned boots with black tassels and toe caps and high heels. The dress with pleats and bustle of the 1870s is not correct for Empress Louise, who would have worn a dress of the Empire period.

14 Bonnet Dolls

These are all German c. 1890. The two smaller dolls are both 8 inches tall and the only marking on their shoulder plates is '5/0'. The doll on the left has a peach coloured bow and green ruching round the bonnet, peach bow under chin and tucking moulded in the shoulder plate. The doll on the right has a white bonnet, the brim lined with blue with a pompon. Both dolls have blue painted eyes and long fair moulded curls.

The larger doll has a pink turban with gold buckle over an adult hairstyle. The painted blue eyes have a red line over. The moulded collar is gold trimmed and there is grey and gold trimming down the front of the shoulder plate. She is wearing original clothes, hand-made cotton underwear and muslin dress. All these dolls have hard, stuffed cotton bodies with tiny waists. There are many varieties of bonnet dolls, the quality of the bisque is not as fine as the earlier bisque but they do have charm.

15 Wax over Composition Dolls (*left*)

The doll on the left is 22 inches tall and was made about 1885. Her papier maché head and shoulders are thickly coated in wax, and she has pale blue paperweight eyes and a brown mohair wig. Her arms and legs are composition and her body is stuffed cotton. She is wearing a blue fine wool tiered dress with silk trimming and a straw bonnet lined to match. Her underwear is original and it includes an unusual blue flannel waist petticoat.

The doll on the right is usually known as a 'Pumpkin Head'. She is 19 inches tall and dates from 1860. Her whole head, with her attractive hairstyle, was modelled in papier maché and thinly coated with wax. She has pupil-less brown glass eyes, wooden spoon hands and wooden legs with painted boots. She has a squeak box inserted in her cloth body which still works. Unlike the earlier wax-over-composition dolls which had their colouring under the wax, these later dolls had their features painted on the wax itself.

16 French Doll: Gesland Body

c. 1865, she is 15 inches tall. The early fashion type bisque head has no maker's mark but it was probably made by F. Gaultier. She is the type sometimes called a 'Parisienne' and has a swivel head on a bisque shoulder plate. Under the elaborately braided real hair wig is a cork pate. The ears are pierced and still have the original earrings. The brows are delicately painted and the glass eyes are outstandingly beautiful and lifelike. The jointed wire body, made by Gesland, a famous Parisian doll-maker, is padded and covered with stockinet. The hands and lower legs are of tinted bisque, and she can assume many positions including kneeling. She would be sold undressed.

17 French Bisque Headed Doll *(left)*

c. 1865, she is also of the type sometimes called a Parisienne or 'Fashion doll'. This is a luxury doll of very fine quality. She is 16 inches tall and her body is made of kid with individually stitched separated fingers. The paperweight eyes are an unusual colour, the iris being grey and white encircled with a deep blue line. The colouring of the face is exceptionally beautiful. She has a swivel neck on a well modelled bisque shoulder plate. Her ears are pierced and she has a wig of real hair. The beautiful dress is in the fashion of the 1870s. Stamped in an oval frame on the front of the kid body is the label of the firm which sold her: 'Au Paradis des Enfants, Perreau Fils, 142 R. Rivoli, R. du Louvre'.

18 Reproduction French Doll

A large number are made today and sold as antique dolls. They are cleverly presented, usually, but not always, on old bodies, with what appears to be the soft dust from a vacuum cleaner blown into their eyes and head to simulate the 'dust of ages'. The eyebrow and mouth painting is not so well done as on the originals and the quality of the bisque is different. This head is of fine quality and is quite well painted and it would be very difficult for anyone who had not handled a number of fashion dolls to recognise this immediately as a fake. The bisque is smoother, like silk, and shows none of the imperfections found in older bisque. The later bisque bébés are also much reproduced and the name stamped on the back of the heads of old dolls is so easily copied that the majority of reproduction dolls are extremely clearly marked. An unmarked genuine doll is always preferable. Old dolls have often lost their name stickers or stamp marks.

31

19 Pedlar Dolls

The one on the left is a wooden doll of c. 1840 wearing a print dress, linen apron, red cloak and black bonnet. She is carrying a well laden tray which includes cards of buttons and needles, minute scissors and spools of cotton, beads, hanks of lace, bags, books and stay laces. This doll is 7½ inches tall.

The pedlar in the middle is 10 inches tall and has a head made of wax with black beady eyes. Under her black bonnet she wears a white lace one, and she is dressed similarly to the other. Her large basket is overflowing with wares, string bags, silk bags, hanks of wool, braid, tapes, pincushions, stay laces, books, cakes of soap in boxes, hat pins, fans, cards of buttons and lace, silver pencil cases, brushes, combs, scissors,

penknife, packets of minute needles and hair pins, and each item is priced. Scented soap is 4d. a cake, silver pencil cases are 6s. 6d. each! She carries a label: 'Licensed to sell small wares'. She is known as 'Sarah Cutler'.

The tiny pedlar is only 6 inches high. She has a dark wax head on a wooden jointed body of c. 1850. She carries a label: 'Licenced Hawker and Dealer in Small Wares'. Note the different spelling. This pedlar is wearing almost identical clothes to the others. Her basket contains sheet music, hand-painted playing cards, ivory articles, sheet of tiny pins, knitted socks and mittens, beaded bags, a tiny basket and a fully-jointed tiny wooden doll.

20 Jumeau Dolls (French)

The doll on the left was made c. 1885. She has large brown stationary glass eyes and a closed mouth. The long blonde wig covers the thick cork pate. On the back of the head is stamped 'Tete Jumeau' in red and the mark on her body is 'Jumeau, Medaille d'or Paris'. She is wearing her original red earrings and shoes with the Jumeau mark on the sole.

The *Jumeau* on the right is known as the 'E.J.'. She is 18 inches tall and has been undressed to show her unusual jointed body. She has ball-joints at shoulder and hip and she has unbroken wrists. The eyes are brown and luminous and the tinted ears are applied and pierced and the delicately painted mouth is closed. The mark on the back of the head is 'Depose E 8 J'. She wears her original Jumeau shoes and socks. The bisque is very pale and the brows not so heavily painted as the previous Jumeau.

The Jumeau firm were making dolls from 1842 until 1899. They had one of the largest doll-making factories in the world and they made all the parts for their dolls as well as their underwear, shoes and socks. The dolls were always of fine quality and they were the luxury dolls of the Victorian well-to-do child.

21 Bru Doll

French c. 1880 this is the most desirable of all dolls to a collector. She is 26 inches tall and has brilliant blue paperweight glass eyes and a closed mouth. The head is very well modelled and is of fine quality bisque. Her kid body is rather plump which suggests she is a child doll and not an adult. Bru dolls are noted for their exquisitely modelled lower arms and hands. The mark on the back of this doll's head is a circle with a dot in the centre which is one of the early trade marks of the Bru company. The mohair wig is thick and curly. She is wearing a lavishly trimmed bonnet and a dark blue silk coat with a green silk lining. Her lace trimmed dress is of blue velvet. The shoes with 'B' on the soles are original Bru shoes. The Bru family were the most inventive of all the doll manufacturers. By 1881 the company had patented twenty-one inventions and had won gold medals at exhibitions all over the world. Bru dolls were known as the most luxurious of all French dolls. The firm made dolls in white and pink kid, porcelain, wood and of jointed rubber. They specialised in 'unbreakable' dolls. The firm was started by Leon Casimir Bru in 1866, his son Casimir Bru Jeune continued with the firm until his death in 1883 when it was taken over by H. Chevrot, but the name 'Bru' remained. Chevrot was succeeded by Paul Eugene Girard as head of Bru Jne & Cie in 1890 and he stayed with the firm until it became part of the *Société Française de Fabrication de Bébés et Jouets* (S.F.B.J.) in 1899.

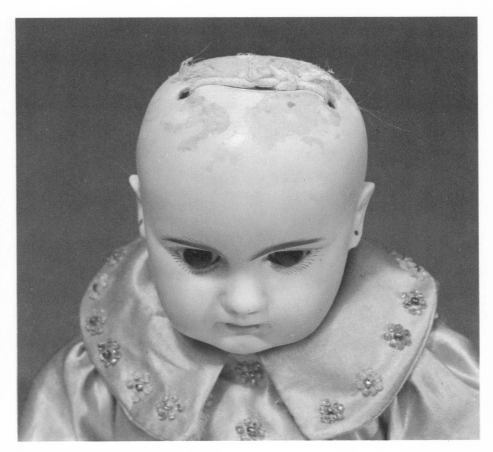

22 Belton Type Bisque Doll

This doll made in 1888 is known as a 'Belton' type. It is difficult to find information about these dolls which are unmarked. The all bisque head is flattened at the top and has two small holes near the front of the head and a larger one behind. This type of doll was often sold with a change of wigs which were attached through the holes in the bisque head. The colouring is very pale with well painted brows and lashes and with brown paperweight eyes. It has a closed mouth and pierced ears. The body is of composition with unjointed wrists and it has a Mama and Papa voice-box operated through strings in the waist.

Belton was a doll-maker in Paris from 1840 and in 1842 he shared an address with Jumeau at 14 Rue Salle au Comte. They were listed as makers of dolls of sheepskin stuffed with sawdust and with china heads. In 1844 Belton and Jumeau received Honourable Mention at the Paris Industries Fair.

24 French Bisque Headed Doll (right)

She has the mark 'F.G.' on the back of the head, which is believed to be the mark of the Gaultier factory. She is 26 inches tall and has very long fair hair. Her brown stationary eyes are large and luminous under heavy brows. She is on a jointed composition body and has very chubby hands. The black leather boots are side buttoning.

This doll called Babette was for many years treasured by Mrs. Laura Treskow who was a founder member of the Doll Club of Great Britain and whose beautiful and unusual dolls have been illustrated in doll books both in this country and the United States. I now have this doll as a constant reminder of a dear and helpful friend who was one of the earliest collectors of antique dolls in England.

23 Bébé Steiner

French 15 inches tall c. 1890. The mark on the back of the head is 'Le Parisien' and on the left side of the body is stamped 'Le petit Parisien, Bébé Steiner'. This extremely pretty doll has blue glass stationary eyes and a real hair wig over a purple cardboard pate. Steiner did not use the cork pates which were the usual head covering among French manufacturers. The colouring of the face is delicate and lifelike. The mouth is closed and the pierced ears are tinted. The hands of the Steiner dolls usually have fingers all of the same length. Another unusual feature of Steiner dolls is that a blue or purple wash appears to have been applied under the paint of their bodies and where the paint has worn off the purple colour shows through.

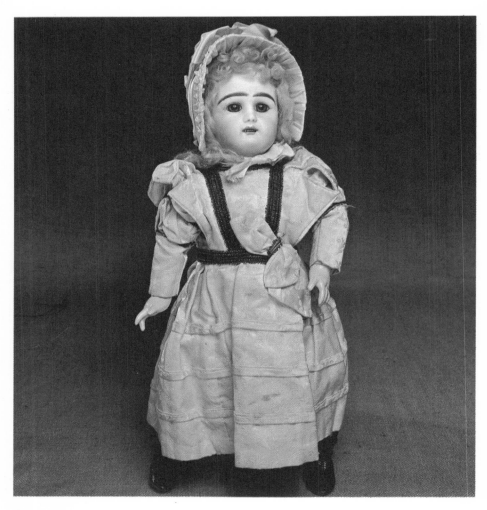

25 Rabery & Delphieu Doll

French bisque headed doll made by Rabery & Delphieu c. 1890. She is 20 inches tall and the mark on the back of her head is 'R 1 D' and 'Rabery Paris' is stamped on her shoes. The stationary grey paperweight glass eyes are large under heavy brows. The open mouth has six porcelain upper teeth. The pull strings in the waist give clearly differentiated Mama and Papa sounds. The blonde mohair wig is nicely styled and the original cork pate is still in the head. The clothes are original throughout, the dress and bonnet being of lemon silk trimmed with braid.

26 French Doll

24½ inches tall this doll was made by A. Lanternier at Limoges c. 1910. The head is of bisque but not of the fine quality of the earlier French dolls, it is rough with many imperfections. The ears are pierced and the blue paperweight eyes are stationary. It has an open mouth with five teeth in a straight line. The wig is made from brown mohair and the jointed body is of wood and composition. This is the mould with 'Cherie' incised on the back of the head and is one of the prettier Limoges dolls. M. Lanternier learned pottery-making at the Wedgwood factory in England.

27 Two French Dolls (*left*)

c. 1900. Both have the mark 'S.F.B.J.' on the back of their heads. The larger doll has a typical Jumeau head with large stationary paperweight eyes and thick cork pate, and she is on a màrked Jumeau body so one can assume she was made very soon after the amalgamation of the French companies.

The smaller doll is more typically the kind we associate with S.F.B.J. She is good quality throughout and has brilliant blue stationary glass eyes. The later dolls made in this mould are of coarser bisque with poorer quality glass eyes, and these were made up to the late 1920s.

28 German Dolls

c. 1895. The larger doll is marked 'Simon & Halbig'. Her head is of good quality bisque and her brilliant blue eyes are of the sleeping type. Her brown mohair wig is original and exactly matches the colour of her well painted eyebrows. She is 22 inches tall.

The smaller doll is very attractively dressed and was made by the firm Schoenau and Hoffmeister. Their trade mark is 'S. (PB in a star) H.' and in the past this manufacturer was often con-fused with Simon and Halbig. This doll has stationary deep blue eyes and her colouring is particularly fine.

43

44

29 German Bisque Doll

Possibly made at the Simon & Halbig factory in the 1880s, the fine bisque head is completely enclosed and she has a swivel neck on a bisque shoulder plate. The brown glass eyes are stationary and the colouring of the face is exceptionally beautiful. The mouth is closed and the long ringlets are of mohair. The wig is glued to the bald head. The kid body is similar to the French fashion type and the lower arms of bisque are well modelled and delicately tinted. She is wearing boots and a brown silk and velvet lace trimmed dress. This doll would be very desirable to a collector, the quality being equal to that of the French dolls of the same period.

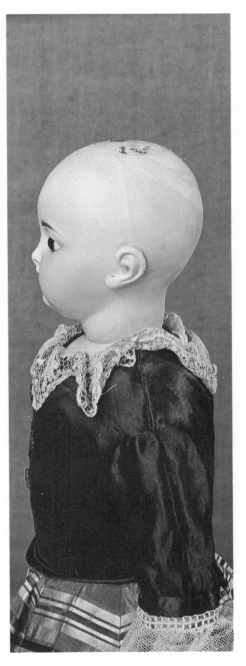

30 German Bisque Head Doll
(left)

On a kid body c. 1890 the head is un-marked but it is probably from the factory of Cuno & Otto Dressel. This is a very pretty doll whose bright blue glass eyes are stationary and her wig is of dark brown mohair. She has a deep dimple in her chin and her lower arms are of delicately tinted and well modelled bisque. The kid body is jointed at the hip. Cuno & Otto Dressel are the oldest recorded doll-makers. The firm was founded in 1700 and continued until 1925.

31 German Bisque Shoulder Head *(right)*

This doll was made by Armand Marseille c. 1895, the mould number is 370 which is the most frequently found of German shoulder heads. The head is glued to a cotton body stuffed with hair and the doll has plaster arms. The brown glass eyes have painted lashes and the wig is of brown mohair. The open mouth dis-plays four porcelain teeth. The clothes are original, hand-sewn cotton under-wear and green print dress trimmed with lace. This head was also used on a kid body, but these are more expensive to buy. The earlier ones are extremely pretty with pale, good quality bisque heads but the later ones are of coarser bisque with a ruddier complexion. Ar-mand Marseille had a porcelain factory in Koppelsdorf in Germany in 1865 and his son, of the same name, made porce-lain dolls' heads there in the 1890s. They were the most prolific makers of dolls' heads, and their prices were sufficiently low for the dolls to be readily available.

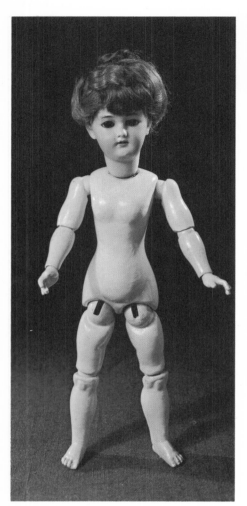

32 German Doll

c. 1907. This 19 inch tall doll is unusual as she is a lady doll and not a child. The bisque head was made by Simon & Halbig, the mould number being 'S.H. 1159'. She has brown glass eyes with lashes and four porcelain teeth. The brown mohair wig is dressed in an up-swept hairstyle. The composition body which has a small waist and a bust was made by the Heinrich Handwerck factory, their name being stamped in purple on the lower body. The Handwerck factory specialised in very good quality ball-jointed dolls and are known to have purchased Simon & Halbig heads for their dolls. Heinrich Handwerck, the founder of the firm, died in 1902 and the factory was taken over by Kammer & Rheinhardt but the firm's name was not changed. This doll was undressed for the photograph to show her body. Her original dress has a bustle and this would be an extremely attractive and unusual doll to have in a collection.

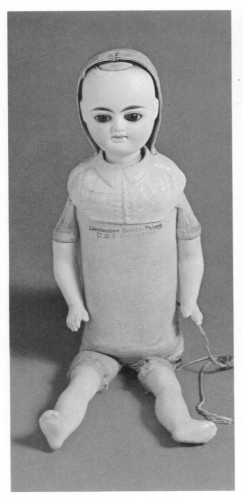
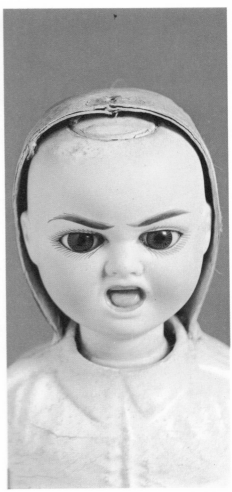

33 Two Faced Doll

A German doll which was made by Fritz Bartenstein at Hüttensteinach c. 1890. It is 15 inches tall and has brown stationary glass eyes. The open/closed mouth has four teeth moulded in the bisque. The face is changed by pulling a string in the waist which works a crying mechanism in the body as the head is changed to the yelling face. The papier maché hood is attached to the shoulder plate which has a collar and frill moulded on. The lower arms and lower legs are of composition. The mark on the body is: 'Deutsches Reichs-Patent, U.S.P. No. 243752'. This is a fine quality doll.

49

34 Three Faced Doll

German c. 1904. This doll is unmarked but was probably made by Carl Bergner who made various types of multi-faced dolls about this period. It is of good quality bisque with brown glass eyes. One face is sleeping, another smiling and the third is crying with very realistic tears moulded in the bisque. The body is similar to the body of the two-faced doll seen on page 49 but it has only one string through the waist which operates the Mama/Papa voice-box. The head is covered with a cardboard hood through which protrudes the knob which is used for changing the faces. The hood is completely covered by a pretty silk bonnet (not shown) which has an opening in the top for the knob. This doll is dressed in a pure silk long gown with flannel and cotton petticoats. This same mould was also used for a doll with a white bisque sleeping face, a mulatto smiling face and a negro crying face. This is much rarer and would be a wonderful addition to any collection.

35 Oriental Girl: Mulatto Boy

Oriental girl doll, c. 1890. There is no mark or maker's name on the back of the head but this attractive and good quality doll is believed to have been made by the Simon & Halbig factory. The doll is 16 inches tall and she is dressed in a silk kimono and she has painted silk shoes with heels. The head is very well modelled and she has dark brown glass eyes and a black real hair wig with pigtail.

The mulatto boy is a good quality French doll about 10 inches tall. There is no maker's name on the doll but the bisque head is of the Belton type with a bald completely enclosed head under the wig of tight black curls. The composition body has jointed legs and stiff slightly bent arms and the doll is strung through the two holes in the top of the head. It is dressed in blue silk tunic and trousers and is wearing 18 carat gold earrings. He would be dated c. 1890.

54

36 Kammer & Reinhardt Dolls

These dolls Peter, mould number 101 c. 1909, and Gretchen, mould number 114, c. 1910, are known as character dolls. Peter has a slender jointed body and Gretchen a chubby one and they are both 20 inches tall. These dolls were modelled by artists from life and they were named after the children who posed for them. The male version of mould 114 is known as Hans and Reinhardt's nephew was the model for this doll. They have well modelled heads and painted blue eyes. Peter is dressed in his original sailor suit and Gretchen is wearing a beautiful dress with frills and tucking. The dolls illustrated are in remarkably good condition and are original throughout. The German factory of Simon & Halbig is believed to have made these character heads for Kammer & Reinhardt. Until 1909, when they brought out the first in their series of character heads, Kammer & Reinhardt had used a single mould for their dolls' heads, one with a little girl type face. The earliest of their character heads was Baby, mould 100. This is the doll which is sometimes called the Kaiser Baby and it was one of the earliest bent limb baby dolls. The others which followed were Marie, Carl, Elise, Walter and Elsa. Kammer & Reinhardt took over the Handwerck factory after the death of Heinrich Handwerck in 1902, so occasionally one finds K & R character heads on a body marked 'Handwerck'. They also made similar dolls' heads in celluloid and these had the turtle trade mark.

These exceptionally fine dolls were kindly loaned by Miss Amy and Miss Muriel Bailey of Richmond, Surrey.

37 Brown Babies

Joey, brown baby, German, c. 1920 is 10 inches tall and was made by the Armand Marseille Company. The mark on the head is 'A.M. 351/2/OK'. The open mouth holds two porcelain bottom teeth. The bisque head is made in the same mould as the very popular English type white baby. Both the white and brown babies were made in all sizes from a few inches to about 34 inches. Coloured dolls were very popular from about 1900 onwards. The composition bodies have bent unjointed limbs, and they have glass sleeping eyes.

The unusually fine English bisque headed brown baby is 20 inches tall. It appears to have been made in the same mould as the German baby dolls. It has brown glass sleeping eyes, two bottom teeth and black painted hair. The mark on the head is 'B.N.D. London'. It is the only doll I have seen with this mark and I have no information about the makers, but it would be dated c. 1912.

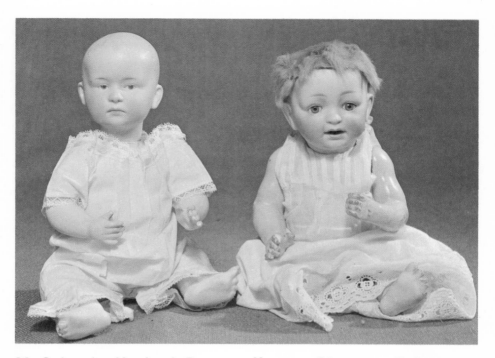

38 Gebruder Heubach Boy

This German boy doll c. 1910 is 14 inches tall. The bisque head has painted hair, a closed mouth and painted intaglio eyes with a white highlight mark at the top of the pupil. This is on a bent limb composition body. Sometimes these heads are on jointed toddler type bodies and the larger heads on the ordinary ball-jointed bodies to represent older boys. A similar mould is used for a shoulder head on a hair stuffed body.

Kestner Character Baby

German c. 1912. This 12 inch long baby has a good quality bisque head with sleeping blue glass eyes which have painted lashes. There are two porcelain teeth in the lower jaw and a moulded bisque tongue. The bent limb composition body is much harder and stronger than the usual baby body, such as the one on the Heubach. The wig is of animal skin with the silky fur brushed in a naturalistic manner to resemble human hair. The pate is not of cardboard as on other German dolls, Kestner used plaster to cover the hole in the top of his dolls' heads. Kestner is believed to be the only German doll-maker who manufactured entire dolls; bodies, heads, eyes, etc., employing almost a thousand workers.

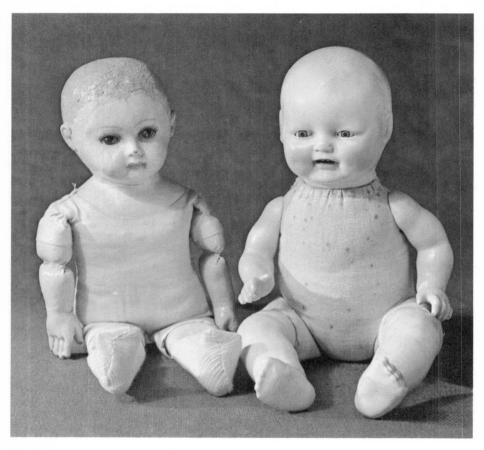

39 American Baby Dolls

Martha Chase Baby Doll, American c. 1900. The head of this doll is made of stockinet which has been glued over a mask which has the features already moulded on, then the head is oil painted so that it is washable. The features are hand-painted and the hair painted in thick strokes. The eyes are painted blue with long lashes. The ears and thumbs were applied separately. This doll has been undressed for the photograph to show its fat cotton body.

It was dressed in its original thin white cotton gown. The legs and arms are oil painted and the name 'Edna' is hand-written on the back of the neck.

Baby Dimples, made in New York by Edward Imeson Horsman c. 1910. A fine quality composition head on a cloth body with tinted composition legs and arms. The doll has sleeping blue glass eyes with painted eyelashes, painted and moulded hair and an open mouth with two teeth at the top.

40 Bye-Lo Baby

American c. 1922. Good quality bisque head with closed mouth on a squat cloth body. It has celluloid hands and blue glass sleeping eyes. The mark on the head is 'COPR. by Grace S. Putnam, Made in Germany'. On the front of the body it is stamped 'Bye-Lo Baby, Pat. appl'd for, copy Grace Storey Putnam'. Grace Storey Putnam was a teacher of art in California and she designed the Bye-Lo baby and Borgfeldt & Company made it in Germany. She spent weeks looking for the 'perfect baby' on which she could model her doll. The Bye-Lo is modelled on a three day old child she found in a hospital in Los Angeles. Later these dolls were made in celluloid, composition, wax, and rubber. This doll was very popular in the United States in the 1920s but they are rare in this country.

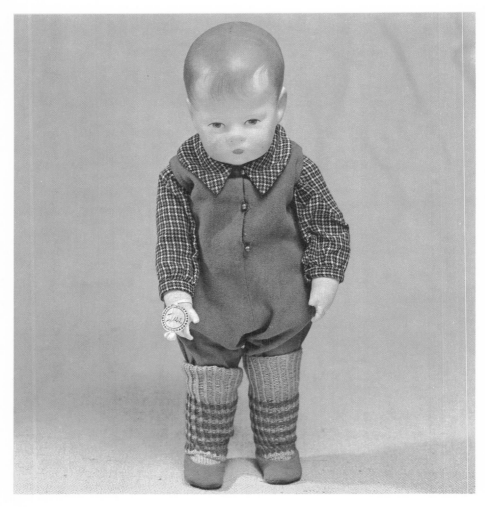

41 Kathe Kruse Boy Doll

German c. 1920. This doll is 19 inches
tall and has the Kathe Kruse label on its
wrist with the mark 'I/122' on the reverse
side. The Kathe Kruse signature is on
the sole of the left foot. The clothes are
original. This doll is in exceptional condition with well painted head and brown
eyes. The whole doll is made of cotton,
the head being treated with chemicals to
stiffen it and then the features are hand-
painted and very lifelike. The Kathe
Kruse factory has been re-opened since
the last war and these beautiful hand-
finished dolls are now being made again.

42 Baby Dolls

Bahr & Proschild German baby doll c. 1910 (left). This doll is 20 inches long and has a very chubby body with bent limbs. It has blue sleeping eyes and a mid-brown mohair wig. Its open/closed mouth has two teeth moulded at the top. It is dressed in pure silk baby clothes and bonnet. Bahr & Proschild had a porcelain factory in Germany from 1871 until 1925. They made china dolls, bisque dolls' heads, figurines and frozen Charlottes.

French Baby made by the S.F.B.J company, mould number 236 (right). This doll is 16 inches long and has brown sleeping eyes and a light brown mohair wig. This doll is one of the most attractive of all baby dolls with its smiling face. It is dressed in long white baby clothes and it still has the label on its back marked 'S.F.B.J. Fabrication Français, Paris'.

44 German Dolls

Simon & Halbig doll (*far right*), mould number 1248. This German doll is 19 inches tall and was made in 1912. She has a wig of fair real hair, blue sleeping eyes and pierced ears. She is wearing her original blue wool dress which is trimmed with lace. This S.H.1248 doll always has unusual mouth shading and is a most attractive little girl type doll.

Kammer & Reinhardt doll (*right*), German c. 1900. This doll is one made from the only mould used by K & R until they brought out their character dolls in 1909. She is 15 inches tall, has blue sleeping eyes and a blonde mohair wig. Her ears are pierced. She is wearing her original shoes and socks and her contemporary clothes were obviously made by a little girl owner who has fastened a gold 'Baby' brooch at her neck.

43 Flirting-Eyed Doll

This doll has a walking mechanism and its right hand comes up to its mouth as it walks to simulate blowing kisses. Its eyes also move from side to side in what is known as a 'flirting' movement. This lovely doll with its brown eyes and brown mohair wig was made by the *Société Française de Fabrication de Bébés et Jouets* which was the company formed by some of the major French doll manufacturers in 1899. Her dress is of pure silk.

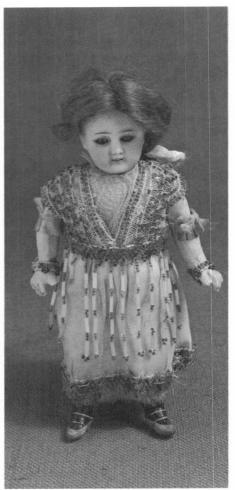

45 French Bisque Head

10 inches tall with the impressed mark 'D' at the back of the head. It has brown glass stationary eyes, dark eyebrows and brown mohair wig. The open mouth has four porcelain teeth at the top. The composition body is of good quality. She is wearing a wool plaid dress and black leather shoes.

46 German Bisque Head

The mark on the back of the head is 'Globe Baby'. Made by Carl Hartmann c. 1898 it has blue glass stationary eyes, painted lashes, open mouth with four teeth, a brown mohair wig and is 9 inches tall. The composition body has straight arms and chubby legs, with painted shoes. Its clothes are original.

47 Dolls with Moulded Hair

Glass-eyed 'Parian' doll. This attractive little doll is 6 inches tall and has brown glass eyes and blonde moulded hair. The bisque is of good quality, the arms and hands being well modelled. The bisque legs have black painted boots which have heels and three straps. The body is made of cotton very tightly stuffed.

The bisque doll (right) has a very attractive high styled arrangement of the moulded hair which is slightly glazed. She is 7 inches tall and has a cloth body with bisque arms and legs which have ribbed stockings and black boots with heels. Her clothes are original. Both are believed to be German, c. 1885.

48 Edwardian Pair

Man doll, 6½ inches tall. The bisque head has a moulded moustache and moulded brown hair. The painted eyes are blue. The head and shoulders are in one piece and the only marks are the numbers '317'. The shoulders are attached to a cloth body with bisque arms and bisque legs which have brown painted shoes with no heels.

Lady doll, 7½ inches tall. The deep shoulder plate has a well modelled bustline and the attached bisque head is bald. The separate wig is of fair mohair with period coiffure. The features are delicately tinted and she has blue painted eyes. The whole arms are of bisque and are attached with wire under the shoulder plate. The hands are beautifully shaped. The cloth body has a tiny waist and the bisque half legs have cream painted stockings and painted brown shoes with blue buckles and with heels. The mark on the shoulder plate is '5568/6'.

49 All Bisque Miniature Dolls

The doll on the left is often called a 'French type' but the country of origin is doubtful. She is $4\frac{1}{2}$ inches tall and with her tight blonde sausage curls she could have been made to be dressed as a boy, but this doll is wearing a frilled print dress and hat. She has deep blue stationary glass eyes and closed mouth. Her painted black shoes have two straps and a small heel.

The middle doll was probably made by Kestner in Germany. She is $3\frac{1}{2}$ inches tall with stationary blue glass eyes, swivel neck, closed mouth and fair mohair wig. She is dressed in a green wool suit and hat and her black painted shoes have a small heel.

The doll on the right is called 'Liane' and was made by J. Verlingue who made dolls in France between 1915 and 1921. His trade mark was an anchor and the initials 'J.V.'. His Paris address was the same as Gesland. This doll is $7\frac{1}{2}$ inches tall with a swivel neck joint protected by a kid lining. She has big brown stationary glass eyes and a long blonde mohair wig. Her legs have painted black boots and white stockings to the knee with a blue garter.

50 Three Dolls of the 1920s

The little girl doll has blue bows moulded
in her blonde hair. She is $4\frac{1}{2}$ inches tall
and is all bisque with wire jointed hips
and shoulders. She has brown painted,
one strap, heel-less shoes. She is one of a
series of dolls of several sizes.

In the centre is a chubby all bisque
baby. She is one of a series which came
in all sizes from 2 to 8 inches tall. The
quality is good and the hair well
moulded with its blue band with a bow.

The 1920s maid doll has a very similar
hair style to the dolls' house dolls of the
1890s. The legs and feet of this doll make
dating easier and the clothes are un-
mistakable.

All three dolls were made in Germany.

51 Four Bisque Dolls

Baby in sitting position (left), German, $2\frac{1}{2}$ inches tall. Painted blonde hair and blue eyes, stiff arms outstretched and bent knees. The bisque is of good quality.

Well modelled girl doll (second left), possibly an early Kestner, $3\frac{1}{2}$ inches tall. She has painted blue eyes and a long blonde mohair wig. The brown shoes have a small heel and two straps and the white ribbed moulded socks have blue tops.

Kewpie type doll, German, $3\frac{1}{2}$ inches tall. The good quality bisque is delicately tinted and she has the mark 'KW1611'. The painted eyes are dark blue. There are blue moulded 'wings' on the shoulders, and a curl of hair at the top of the head, at the sides, at the nape of the neck and on the forehead. Kewpie dolls were designed by Mrs. Rose O'Neill Wilson and the name was registered as a trade mark in the United States, Britain and France in 1913. This attractive little doll was kindly loaned to me by Miss Wendy Wymark, a little Australian friend, who at eight years old must be one of the youngest collectors of antique dolls.

Snow baby (right), German, $4\frac{1}{2}$ inches tall. Good quality bisque. The ski stick is missing. The snow babies were made in many sizes and positions and were used primarily as cake decorations.

52 Miniature Dolls

All have bisque heads and composition bodies. The doll on the left is 5 inches tall. She has blue glass stationary eyes with exaggerated painted eyelashes. Open mouth with two porcelain teeth. Her long hair is in a plait. She has black painted socks and two-strap shoes. Her dress, bonnet and cape are in· crochet. She is holding an all bisque doll, $1\frac{1}{2}$ inches tall, dressed as a baby.

The centre doll is $4\frac{1}{2}$ inches tall. She has a closed mouth and deep blue sleeping eyes. Her very fashionable outfit is hand-made and lavishly trimmed with lace.

The little coloured doll is 4 inches tall. She was made by Simon & Halbig. She has a black curly mohair wig.

These were made in Germany, c. 1890.

53 Frozen Charlottes

These unjointed china dolls are also
called pudding dolls, bathing babies and
pillar dolls and they were made from
1850 up to 1914. The ones illustrated are
all of glazed porcelain, but sometimes
one finds similar unglazed dolls. Some
are of superb quality with pink tinted
(known as 'pink lustre') bodies and
heads. The hairstyles vary and some
have bonnets moulded on and some
have moulded dresses. They were made
in sizes from $\frac{3}{4}$ inch up to 18 inches. The
name is taken from a New England bal-
lad of about 1830 called 'Fair Charlotte'
about a beautiful and vain young
maiden who insisted on going for a
sleigh ride in the snow with no blanket,
so that she could show off her beautiful
gown.

There are twenty-one verses to this
ballad but the last two are:

> He took her hand into his own,
> Oh God! It was cold as stone.
> He tore her mantle from her brow
> On her face the cold stars shone.
>
> Then quickly to the lighted hall
> Her lifeless form he bore,
> Fair Charlotte was a frozen corpse,
> And her lips spake nevermore.

54 A Dolls' House Family

The two most interesting dolls are the man doll and the lady doll in the green silk wrap on the right. These are lustre china dolls on jointed wooden bodies and were made about 1845.

The small girl with the long blonde ringlets is of exceptional quality for such a small doll, she is only $3\frac{3}{4}$ inches tall and has her original cream silk dress. The 'mother' doll with the moulded hair piled high on the head is dressed in an original grey silk dress and velvet jacket. Other dolls which are available to complete the household would be grandmother, grandfather with his bald head and side whiskers, butler and groom. Male dolls are not easy to find so there is usually a majority of females in a dolls' house population.

55 A Street of Dolls' Houses

These are all 'for sale' except Rodmore House on the right. They are the smaller houses which can be hung on a wall or kept on an eye-level shelf.

These Victorian houses bear the original paint but need restoration.

The first house (*left*) is 22 inches high, 11 inches wide and 6 inches deep. It is the earliest house here, possibly c. 1845, and contains two rooms with fireplaces set in a chimney breast. The front opens, and there are green painted Venetian blinds on the windows.

The next house is 18 inches high, 17½ inches wide and 10 inches deep and opens at the back. It has two rooms with fireplaces and a staircase with landing.

The centre house with steps leading to the front door is 20 by 20 by 11 inches.

The fireplaces and fenders are original.

The fourth is three-storeyed and is 25 by 11 by 10 inches. It has a wooden balcony and an unusual number of windows, each floor having two long ones on both sides. I feel the top floor was an afterthought but can find no join in the wood. This would make a fine town house.

'Rodmore House', a typical Victorian villa, is 29 by 17 by 14 inches. The front opens to reveal two rooms with fireplaces. The attic is reached from the back.

56 Miniature Dolls' House

57 Interior

This perfect tiny house, which is 16″ high, 9″ wide and 4½″ deep, was made by a father and lovingly furnished by the mother and daughters of the family. It is beautifully made and to almost faultless scale. It is very attractive when closed and would make an excellent house for hanging on a wall.

The entrance hall has a parquet floor and imposing staircase. The drawing room windows are built with mirror behind which gives an illusion of depth and a view beyond. The elegantly dressed lady in this room is only 1½″ tall. This household also has pets without which no Victorian dolls' house would be complete.

74

58 Victorian Dolls' House

Height 47 inches, width 41 inches, depth 14 inches. This family house with its lace curtains preserving the privacy of its occupants was completely empty when it was bought. The paintwork on the outside is original, with the markings for the bricks scored in the paint. The front opens to reveal five rooms furnished with great care and attention to detail and with great taste. The drawing room is elegantly furnished with French furniture and the furniture in the rest of the house is mostly 'Duncan Phyfe'. All the rooms except the kitchen have chandeliers and in the spacious hall is a 'Duncan Phyfe' bookcase containing a library of real miniature books. The contemporary bathroom is a feature of this home. There are fifteen small dolls in the house—the family includes twin children and there are also visiting relatives and of course, the staff, without which no middle class Victorian home was complete. Every room is arranged

as an interesting scene, from the cook in the kitchen preparing a meal for the large family to the child being bathed and prepared for bed. An aunt is sitting at the grand piano and it looks as if 'papa' is leaving the house, possibly to take a short walk before sitting down to a dinner of many courses.

This house was kindly loaned by Mrs. Joan Hunter of Twickenham who has spent five very enjoyable years collecting to bring this house to near perfection.

59 Penrhyn House

This once belonged to Lord Penrhyn and his sisters and is now known to the new owner as 'Penrhyn House'. This most charming house is 40 inches high, 28 inches wide and 14½ inches deep. The coach house, now converted to a boathouse, is 20 inches high, 12 inches wide and 8½ inches deep. The garden is 15 inches by 27½ inches. The outside paint is all original and the roofs are papered. The tastefully furnished rooms have their original wallpapers. There are many treasures in this house which have taken months of patient searching to obtain. The dining table has solid silver appointments including a miniature entrée dish. The drawing room has a suite of fine quality 'inlaid' furniture, a chess table, a pair of Sèvres vases and a fine chandelier. The family includes, mother, father, grandmother and grandfather, six children and two maids. Four of the children are having tea in the garden and there is a boneshaker propped against the wall. There is also a playroom above the coach house, which now houses a skiff. This is an exceptionally attractive house with its lovely garden and the unusual addition of the coach house. It was kindly loaned by Mrs. William Griffith of Kensington, who has now started the formidable task of furnishing her newly acquired Georgian baby house.

79

DOLL COLLECTIONS

Most museums have something to offer to the collector of dolls and dolls' houses, but the few listed below I have visited and enjoyed. There are, of course, many hundreds of superb collections in America and all over the world, which I look forward to visiting.

BOWES MUSEUM, Barnard Castle, Co. Durham
PENRHYN CASTLE, Bangor, North Wales
MUSEUM OF COSTUME, Bath
CITY MUSEUM, Birmingham
BLAISE CASTLE, Bristol
MUSEUM OF CHILDHOOD, Edinburgh
CARLISLE MUSEUM, Carlisle
PENSHURST PLACE, Near Tunbridge Wells, Kent
TUNBRIDGE WELLS MUSEUM, Tunbridge Wells
WINDSOR CASTLE, Windsor

BARRY ELDER DOLL MUSEUM, Carr House, Bretherton, Nr. Preston, Lancs.
HARRIS MUSEUM, Preston
ABBEY HOUSE MUSEUM, Leeds
BETHNAL GREEN MUSEUM, London
LONDON MUSEUM, Kensington
POLLOCKS TOY MUSEUM, Scala Street, London
LUTON MUSEUM, Luton
ROTUNDA, Grove House, Iffley Turn, Near Oxford
GRANGE TOY MUSEUM, Rottingdean, Sussex
MUSEUM OF CHILDHOOD AND COSTUME, Blithfield Hall, Rugeley, Staffs.
SALISBURY MUSEUM, Salisbury
SOMERSET COUNTY MUSEUM, Taunton
DOLL MUSEUM, Warwick
WORTHING MUSEUM, Worthing
RINGWOOD TOY MUSEUM, Ringwood, Hants.
CASTLE MUSEUM, York

BIBLIOGRAPHY

COLEMAN Dorothy, *The Collector's Encyclopedia of Dolls*, Crown, USA 1968
EARLY Alice K., *English Dolls, Effigies & Puppets*, Batsford, UK 1955
FAWCETT Clara H., *Dolls, A New Guide for Collectors*, Branford, USA: Bailey Bros., UK 1964
GERKEN Jo E., *Wonderful Dolls of Wax*
GREENE Vivien, *English Dolls' Houses*, Batsford, UK 1955
HILLIER Mary, *Dolls and Dollmakers*, Weidenfeld & Nicolson, UK 1968: Putnam, USA 1968

JACOBS F. G. & FAURHOLT E. *A Book of Dolls and Dolls Houses*, C. E. Tuttle, USA 1967
JOHNSON Audrey, *How to Repair and Dress Old Dolls*, G. Bell, UK 1967: Branford, USA 1967
JOHNSON Audrey, *Dressing Dolls*, G. Bell, UK 1969: Branford, USA 1969
LATHAM Jean, *Dolls' Houses, A Personal Choice*, A. & C. Black, UK 1969; Scribner, USA 1969
NOBLE John, *Dolls*, Walker & Co., New York, 1967; Studio Vista, UK 1968
ST. GEORGE Eleanor, *Old Dolls*, Bonanza, New York; B.S.C. Books, UK 1969